**NEW Spirals**

# Dribs and Drabs

### Chris Culshaw

Text © Chris Culshaw 2004

The right of Chris Culshaw to be identified as the author of this work has been asserted by him in accordance with the Copyright, Designs and Patents Act 1988.

All rights reserved. No part of this publication may be reproduced or transmitted in any form or by any means, electronic or mechanical, including photocopy, recording or any information storage and retrieval system, without permission in writing from the publisher or under licence from the Copyright Licensing Agency Limited, 90 Tottenham Court Road, London W1T 4LP.

Any person who commits any unauthorised act in relation to this publication may be liable to criminal prosecution and civil claims for damages.

Published in 2004 by:
Nelson Thornes Ltd
Delta Place
27 Bath Road
CHELTENHAM
GL53 7TH
United Kingdom

04 05 06 07 08 / 10 9 8 7 6 5 4 3 2 1

A catalogue record for this book is available from the British Library

ISBN 0-7487-9012-8

Cover illustration by Rupert Besley
Page make-up by Tech-Set, Gateshead

Printed in Croatia by Zrinski

# Contents

Three short plays for three parts.

## Mates R Us _____ 4

3 parts:  *R. Dribs* (male or female)
  *R. Drabs* (male or female)
  *Mr. Roll*

## Ghosts R Us _____ 15

3 parts:  *R. Dribs* (male or female)
  *R. Drabs* (male or female)
  *Chris Cross* (male or female)

## Ashes R Us _____ 24

3 parts:  *R. Dribs* (male or female)
  *R. Drabs* (male or female)
  *Mrs Wright*

# Mates R Us

3 parts: Dribs: Owner of **Mates R Us** dating agency
Drabs: Dribs's useless assistant
Mr Roll: a customer

*Scene: The office of Mates R Us. A customer enters, looking nervous*

| | |
|---|---|
| *Dribs* | Good morning. |
| *Mr Roll* | [*Looking round*] Are we alone? **She's** not here, is she? |
| *Drabs* | She? No. |
| *Mr Roll* | She said she was on her way. |
| *Drabs* | Who? |
| *Dribs* | Come in. There's no one here. Don't be shy. Sit down. First time? |
| *Mr Roll* | No. I sat down earlier. |
| *Dribs* | Just relax. Now then, how can we help? |
| *Drabs* | 'For a date or a mate<br>You don't have to wait.<br>Try Dribs and Drabs<br>For love on a plate!' |
| *Mr Roll* | That sounds promising. |
| *Dribs* | You've come to the right place if you're looking for the woman of your dreams. |

| | |
|---|---|
| *Mr Roll* | I've just left the one of my nightmares. |
| *Drabs* | With our new laser software we can find a perfect match for any customer. |
| *Dribs* | I've got a huge database. |
| *Mr Roll* | Can't you get tablets for that? |
| *Drabs* | We'll need to enter some data. There are a few questions for you to answer. |
| *Dribs* | All very simple. Just relax. |
| *Drabs* | Question one – clothes. What is your style? Er . . . I see you're wearing one black shoe and one white shoe. |
| *Mr Roll* | That's odd. I've got another pair just like that at home. |
| *Drabs* | They're on the wrong feet. |
| *Mr Roll* | I had my legs crossed when I put them on. |
| *Dribs* | [*To Drabs*] Go and make some tea. [*To Mr Roll*] Just try to relax. We're here to help. [*Drabs exits*] |
| *Mr Roll* | I've never been to a place like this before. |
| *Dribs* | No problem. So you're looking for a wife, eh? |
| *Mr Roll* | Yes. I used to have one but she was scary. |
| *Drabs* | [*Putting his head round the door*] One lump or two? |

| | |
|---|---|
| *Mr Roll* | Hundreds. She had lumps all over. |
| *Drabs* | No. How many lumps in your **tea**? |
| *Mr Roll* | I don't like lumpy tea. |
| *Drabs* | Sugar. How much sugar, you great big . . . |
| *Dribs* | [*Slamming the door in Drabs's face*] Go on. You were saying about your last wife. |
| *Mr Roll* | She was a very bad cook. Even the mice went next door for supper. |
| *Dribs* | Try to relax. You seem very tense. |
| *Mr Roll* | So would you be if you'd been married to that woman. |
| *Dribs* | Your hands are shaking. I see you bite your nails. |
| *Drabs* | [*Putting head round the door*] Chocolate fingers? |
| Mr. Roll | No, they're normal. |
| *Drabs* | Or a custard cream. There's just the one. The mice ate the rest. |
| *Dribs* | [*Slamming the door in Drabs's face again*] So you're looking for a new wife, are you? |
| *Mr Roll* | Yes. I tried putting an advert in the local paper. |
| *Dribs* | What did you write? |
| *Mr Roll* | Simple. 'Wife wanted.' |

| | |
|---|---|
| *Dribs* | Did you get many replies? |
| *Mr Roll* | Hundreds. They all said the same thing: 'You can have mine.' |
| *Drabs* | [*Enters with tea*] Help yourself. |
| *Mr Roll* | They said that as well. |
| *Drabs* | No, the tea. |
| *Dribs* | I'll type in your details. Name? |
| *Mr Roll* | Roll. |
| *Drabs* | First name? |
| *Mr Roll* | Egbert. But everybody calls me Egg, for a joke. |
| *Drabs* | Middle name? |
| *Mr Roll* | Chris. |
| *Dribs* | [*Types at keyboard*] 'Egg and Chris Roll.' |
| *Drabs* | Yes please. With mustard. |
| *Dribs* | Where were you born, Mr Roll? |
| *Mr Roll* | In the Alps. |
| *Drabs* | Then you must be a Swiss roll! |
| *Dribs* | What's your birth sign? |
| *Mr Roll* | Pardon? |
| *Dribs* | What sign were you born under? |
| *Mr Roll* | [*Thinking hard*] It was green and said: 'Ward 6.' |

| | |
|---|---|
| *Dribs* | No. What **star** sign? |
| *Mr Roll* | Oh that. Leo, the Leopard. |
| *Drabs* | Are you sure? |
| *Mr Roll* | Yes, I had lots of spots as a baby. My mum could spot me a mile off. |
| *Dribs* | Have you had many girl friends? |
| *Mr Roll* | I was engaged to a girl with a wooden leg called Kate. |
| *Drabs* | What was her other leg called? |
| *Mr Roll* | But we didn't get on and she broke it off. |
| *Drabs* | Ouch. A snap decision, eh? |
| *Mr Roll* | And then I went out with the girl next door. |
| *Dribs* | The cute girl from next door, eh? |
| *Mr Roll* | No, she was dead ugly. |
| *Drabs* | So why did you go out with her? |
| *Mr Roll* | It was cheap. We didn't go out much. She only lived next door. I saved loads on taxi fares. |
| *Dribs* | Did you never see her home? |
| *Mr Roll* | Yeah – I just looked out of the window and there it was. |
| *Drabs* | So did you become close? |
| *Mr Roll* | Very close. Like I say, she was just next door. |

| | |
|---|---|
| *Dribs* | But you didn't marry her? |
| *Mr Roll* | No. It wouldn't have worked out. |
| *Dribs* | Why's that? |
| *Mr Roll* | We were only ten at the time. I told her I'd go to the end of the world for her. |
| *Dribs* | What did she say? |
| *Mr Roll* | 'Good-bye then.' She used to wear a faint perfume. |
| *Drabs* | How faint? |
| *Mr Roll* | One sniff and I fainted. |
| *Dribs* | I like that perfume called Tornado. |
| *Mr Roll* | Nice smell? |
| *Drabs* | No, but it blows the flies away. There's your tea. |
| *Mr Roll* | Should it be that colour? |
| *Drabs* | It's the milk. |
| *Dribs* | What about the milk? |
| *Drabs* | There isn't any. |
| *Dribs* | I've got milk in mine. |
| *Drabs* | It was the last few drops. From the cat's bowl. |
| *Dribs* | Right. So you've been unlucky in love, Mr Roll? |

| | |
|---|---|
| *Mr Roll* | True. There was the girl at the gym. When she did a back flip and a forward roll I fell head over heels in love with her. |
| *Dribs* | Was it love at first sight? |
| *Mr Roll* | Yes. The trouble was, she took a second look. |
| *Dribs* | Did she make a good impression on you? |
| *Mr Roll* | Yes. She did bird impressions, you see. |
| *Drabs* | How clever. |
| *Mr Roll* | She watched me like a hawk. |
| *Drabs* | That must have been hard to swallow. |
| *Mr Roll* | Yes. But I used to do animal impressions for her. Any farm animal she could name. |
| *Dribs* | That must have been noisy. |
| *Mr Roll* | Not really. I only did the smells. |
| *Drabs* | What's your job? |
| *Mr Roll* | All sorts. I was a bus driver once. It was great. |
| *Dribs* | What did you like about being a bus driver? |
| *Mr Roll* | Telling people where to get off. |
| *Drabs* | Fare enough! I'm a very good driver. I always look both ways before I hit something. |
| *Dribs* | Tell us about your wife. |

| | |
|---|---|
| *Mr Roll* | Ah yes. My late wife. |
| *Dribs* | I'm sorry to hear she died. |
| *Mr Roll* | She didn't. She's alive and well. It's just that she can never get anywhere on time. |
| *Drabs* | Is that why you split up? |
| *Mr Roll* | Not really. She was only half my size. |
| *Dribs* | What's that got to do with it? |
| *Mr Roll* | We could never see eye to eye. |
| *Drabs* | How long were you married? |
| *Mr Roll* | Two weeks. |
| *Drabs* | Two weeks? |
| *Mr Roll* | The honeymoon finished us off. We had a hotel with a balcony. But we could never agree on the balcony. |
| *Dribs* | You could never agree on the balcony? |
| *Mr Roll* | No. We kept falling out over it. |
| *Drabs* | That's the trouble with balconies. |
| *Mr Roll* | I promised her the time of her life. But the hotel was awful. It was very cheap. |
| *Dribs* | What was wrong with it? |
| *Mr Roll* | I rang room service and asked them to send up a towel. They said: 'Sorry. Someone's using it at the moment.' |

| | |
|---|---|
| *Drabs* | So your new wife wasn't happy. |
| *Mr Roll* | She left the next day. |
| *Dribs* | How sad. Anyway, we need to tell the computer about your talents. Can you cook? |
| *Mr Roll* | I can boil a kettle and warm the plates. |
| *Drabs* | Nothing fancy, then? |
| *Mr Roll* | I can make soup. Thick soup. It's so thick that when I stir it, the room goes round. |
| *Dribs* | What about dancing? |
| *Mr Roll* | No thanks I've just had breakfast. |
| *Dribs* | I mean can you dance? Are you dynamite at a disco? |
| *Mr Roll* | More like a Scud missile. I can jig. I met a girl at an Irish dance only last week. |
| *Drabs* | Oh really. |
| *Mr Roll* | No, O'Reilly. |
| *Dribs* | What happened? |
| *Mr Roll* | I asked her if I could see her home . . . |
| *Dribs* | . . . And? |
| *Mr Roll* | She showed me a picture of her flat in Dublin. |
| *Dribs* | Was she nice? |

| | |
|---|---|
| *Mr Roll* | Very. But I put my foot right in it. I said her tights looked wrinkled. |
| *Dribs* | So? |
| *Mr Roll* | She wasn't wearing any. |
| *Dribs* | Oh dear! |
| *Drabs* | Did you ask her to marry you? |
| *Mr Roll* | Yes. But her family said no. |
| *Drabs* | Her family? |
| *Mr Roll* | Yes, her husband and two kids. |
| *Drabs* | I think I'd better go and wash up. I don't think we're getting very far. |
| *Dribs* | Pipe down you. It's fine. We're nearly there. I just need to tell the computer what you look like. |
| *Drabs* | This is where it might crash. |
| *Dribs* | Shhhhh. Okay. I've put in all your details. Now it's thinking. |
| *Mr Roll* | It's taking a long time. |
| *Drabs* | It's got a lot to think about. In fact it may be having a nervous break down. |
| *Dribs* | Quiet. Relax. Here comes the print-out. |
| *Mr Roll* | It's making a funny noise. |
| *Drabs* | It does that sometimes. When it laughs. |

| | |
|---|---|
| *Dribs* | Shhhhh. It's fine. Just relax. Here it comes. |
| *Drabs* | You're in luck. It's found the perfect match. |
| *Dribs* | [*Hands Mr Roll the print-out*] Here's her photograph, and her name and all her details. |
| *Mr Roll* | Let me see. [*Excited*] Who's the lucky woman? |
| *Drabs* | She looks very nice. |
| *Dribs* | She looks just your sort. |
| *Mr Roll* | Oh no! I don't believe it. |
| *Dribs* | What's the matter? |
| *Drabs* | Do you know her? |
| *Mr Roll* | Know her! Know her! It's the woman who divorced me six months ago! |

# Ghosts R Us

3 parts: Dribs: the guide and owner of Haunted Hikes
Drabs: a 'ghost' who works for Dribs – draped in a sheet
Chris Cross: a customer

*Scene: A grave-yard at midnight*

| | |
|---|---|
| *Dribs* | Welcome to Haunted Hikes. [*A clock strikes twelve*] Ah, midnight – the twitching hour. Just right for your Spooks Tour with 'Ghosts R Us'. |
| *Chris Cross* | [*Looking around nervously*] Am I the **only** customer? |
| *Dribs* | Yes. DEAD right! |
| *Chris Cross* | How long is this hike? |
| *Dribs* | A couple of KILL-ometres. |
| *Chris Cross* | Will we see any ghosts tonight? |
| *Dribs* | Lots. You'll be DYING to see them. |
| *Chris Cross* | [*Screaming*] Woooooo! Oooh! |
| *Dribs* | What's the matter? I can't see any ghosts yet. |
| *Chris Cross* | You're standing on my foot. |
| *Drabs* | [*Hiding behind a grave stone*] Woooooooooooohhhh . . . . . . . . . . . Whooooooo areeeee youoooooooooooo? |

| | |
|---|---|
| *Chris Cross* | [*Hanging on Dribs's arm*] Whhhhattt wwwwas thhthaat? |
| *Dribs* | That was the ghost of Richard the Third. Or it might have been Henry the Eighth. I was never any good at fractions. |
| *Drabs* | [*Appears slowly from behind a gravestone. Sounding very bored*] Gooooood eveninnnnnng. This is the ghooooost of Henry the Eighth. Welcooooome to the ghooooool's graveyard, the dead centre of toooown. |
| *Dribs* | [*Whispers to Drabs*] Put a bit of life into it, Drabs. You sound half-dead. |
| *Drabs* | [*Whispers*] That's how I feel. I've been sitting on that grave for three hours. I've got a rumbling tum, a grumbling thumb and a numb bum, chum. By gum, I'm glum. |
| *Chris Cross* | [*Nervous*] Are you **really** a ghost? One of the living dead? |
| *Drabs* | Dead as a Doooo-Dooooo. |
| *Dribs* | [*Angrily whispers to Drabs*] Where are the others? I told you to hire three more skeletons. |
| *Drabs* | [*Whispers*] They're on strike. I'm their spooks-person. We all want a pay rise. This is a dead-end job. |

| | |
|---|---|
| *Dribs* | Pipe down! Spook when you're spoken to. And stop picking your nose under that sheet. |
| *Drabs* | Why? I'm a bogeyman, aren't I? |
| *Chris Cross* | You don't sound very scary to me. |
| *Drabs* | [*To Dribs*] I want a pay rise. |
| *Chris Cross* | [*Overhears*] Pay rise? What do you mean? Ghosts don't get paid. |
| *Drabs* | This one does. |
| *Dribs* | Shut up, you fool. You'll ruin everything. |
| *Drabs* | And we want danger money. One of the skeletons was attacked by a dog last week. It ran off with a bone. Now he hasn't a leg to stand on. |
| *Chris Cross* | [*Lifting Drabs's sheet*] You're no ghost! Talking of legs, if you're the ghost of Henry the Eighth, how come you're wearing trainers? |
| *Drabs* | They're not trainers. They're bowling shoes. |
| *Chris Cross* | Why would King Henry wear bowling shoes? |
| *Drabs* | They were a present from Anne *Bowlin*. |
| *Chris Cross* | This tour is one big con. I paid good money to see skeletons climbing out of their coffins. |

17

| | |
|---|---|
| *Dribs* | Sorry – they're all locked in for the night. |
| *Drabs* | But they've got skeleton keys! |
| Chris Cross | This **is** a con. You're not a real ghost. You're just hiding under a bed sheet. You don't scare me. I want my money back – **now**. |
| *Drabs* | [*Trying hard to be scary*] Wooooooooooo! |
| Chris Cross | [*Angry*] Very scary, I don't say! I could do better than that. |
| *Drabs* | Don't blame me. Don't be cross. |
| Chris Cross | Of course I'm cross. I'm always cross. |
| *Dribs* | Why's that? |
| Chris Cross | It's my name. I'm Chris Cross. |
| *Dribs* | Chris Cross? |
| *Drabs* | Chris Cross? |
| *Dribs* | That sounds like a row of kisses! |
| Chris Cross | I'm Chris Cross from the X files. I'm here to investigate things that aren't normal. |
| *Drabs* | What a cheek! I'm very normal. [*Removes the sheet to show a black eye*] I've had enough. I quit. |
| Chris Cross | Ughhhhhh! Where did you get that mask? It's horrible. |
| *Drabs* | I'm not wearing a mask. |

| | |
|---|---|
| *Chris Cross* | How did you get that black eye? |
| *Drabs* | See that tree over there? |
| *Chris Cross* | Yes. |
| *Drabs* | Well I didn't. |
| *Chris Cross* | [*Picking up the sheet*] This is a hospital sheet. Look, the label says: 'Maternity Ward.' |
| *Drabs* | I went in for a face-lift. |
| *Dribs* | But they found another one just as bad underneath. |
| *Chris Cross* | So you stole this sheet, did you? |
| *Drabs* | No. I'm a doctor. |
| *Dribs* | Known in the trade as a surgical spirit! |
| *Chris Cross* | Anyone could do this job. Even me. I need a new job. [*Getting under the sheet*] Let me try. It can't be that hard. Wooooooooooo. Arrrrrrrrr. Hoooooooooo. How's that? |
| *Drabs* | [*Laughing*] What do you call that? You sound like a cat sitting on a thistle with a wasp up its nose. |
| *Dribs* | [*To Chris Cross*] Not bad! Have you ever done any acting? |
| *Chris Cross* | You might have seen me in the movies. |

19

| | |
|---|---|
| *Drabs* | Yeah – kissing in the back row! |
| *Dribs* | [*To Chris Cross*] Would you like the job? |
| *Drabs* | Just a minute! You can't do that. Anyone who does this job has to belong to the Union of Spooks and Ghouls – USAG. |
| *Chris Cross* | You what? |
| *Drabs* | USAG. |
| *Dribs* | You sag! |
| *Drabs* | No I don't. I've just had a face-lift. |
| *Chris Cross* | I'd like to join 'Ghosts R Us'. I'm a great actor. And actors like me don't grow on trees. |
| *Drabs* | No, they **swing** from them. You need brains to be a spook. |
| *Chris Cross* | I'm smarter than I look. |
| *Drabs* | You need to be. |
| *Dribs* | What kind of spooks can you do? |
| *Drabs* | I bet you haven't got the guts to be a skeleton. |
| *Chris Cross* | What about a headless ghost? |
| *Drabs* | Good idea. I'll get an axe. |
| *Chris Cross* | Or I could act invisible and tell people I'm the head of King Charles. |

| | |
|---|---|
| *Drabs* | No – they'd see right through you. |
| *Dribs* | I'll give you a trial. If you do a good job, you can work for 'Ghosts R Us'. |
| *Chris Cross* | What's the pay? |
| *Dribs* | Ten pence a fright. The more you scare, the more you earn. Think you can handle it? |
| *Drabs* | What about me? |
| *Dribs* | Whoever's the scariest gets to be the top ghost. That's fair, isn't it? Show me what you can do. |
| *Drabs* | I've got grave doubts. Ha – get the joke? |
| *Chris Cross* | I'm in tomb-minds whether to do this. Get it? |
| *Dribs* | I don't want jokes. I want frights. |
| *Chris Cross* | You might get more customers with a few jokes. |
| *Drabs* | Yeah – so far we've only had dribs and drabs! |
| *Dribs* | In that case I'll pretend to be a customer. You two hide. I'll count to three, then you jump out and try to scare me. |
| | *[Chris Cross and Drabs go off to hide. Dribs sits on a gravestone and counts to three. An owl hoots. It is deathly still.]* |

| | |
|---|---|
| *Chris Cross* | [*Leaping up with a blood-curdling voice*] |
| | I am the ghost of Jack the Ripper |
| | With the smell of death – a bit like a kipper. |
| | Beware of Jack the Ripper's ghost . . . |
| | I'll chop you up and eat you on toast. |
| | Arrrrrrrrrgh!  Oooohhhhhhhhhh. |
| *Dribs* | Not bad.  Not bad. |
| *Chris Cross* | Have I got the job then? |
| *Dribs* | Let's see what Drabs can do.  [*Looking round*] Drabs, where are you? |
| *Chris Cross* | What was that? |
| *Dribs* | What? |
| *Chris Cross* | Over there.  By that cross. |
| *Dribs* | What is it? |
| *Chris Cross* | A shape. |
| *Dribs* | Did you just feel an icy shiver? |
| *Chris Cross* | It shot down my neck. |
| *Dribs* | It ran up my spine. |
| *Chris Cross* | Maybe I don't want this job after all. |
| *Dribs* | Come on, Drabs.  Let's go home. [*Pause*] Drabs?  Where are you? |
| *Chris Cross* | Ssssh.  There's something over there. |

| | |
|---|---|
| *Dribs* | Where? I can't see a thing. It's pitch black. |
| *Chris Cross* | Over there, by that old twisted tree. |
| *Dribs* | What is it? |
| *Chris Cross* | A face. An ugly, terrible face. |
| *Dribs* | That'll be Drabs. |
| *Chris Cross* | But it's covered in blood. |
| *Dribs* | I want to go home. |
| *Chris Cross* | There's a huge vampire with fangs . . . It's holding a long knife in one hand and a head in the other. It's coming this way . . . |
| *Dribs* | That head looks familiar. |
| *Chris Cross* | It's got a black eye! |
| *Dribs* | The vampire is lifting the head in the air. |
| *Chris Cross* | It's giving it another face-lift. |
| *Dribs* | Oh no! Poor Drabs . . . |
| *Chris Cross* | Ooh – you said you wanted a fright . . . |
| *Dribs* | Not like this, I didn't. |
| *Chris Cross* | You were looking for a scare – well now you've found one . . . |
| *Dribs* | It's Dracula himself! Arrrrggghhhhhhhh! |

[*They both run off . . . screaming*]

# Ashes R Us

3 parts:  Dribs: the boss of Ashes R Us
         Drabs: Dribs's useless assistant
         Mrs Wright: a customer

*Scene: The office of Ashes R Us*

| | |
|---|---|
| *Dribs* | What am I going to tell her? You idiot! |
| *Drabs* | It isn't my fault. |
| *Dribs* | Of course it's your fault. I paid you to do the job. What are we going to say? |
| *Drabs* | I'll think of something. |
| *Dribs* | No you won't. Let me handle this. |
| *Mrs Wright* | [*Enters*] Good day. |
| *Drabs* | Good morning. |
| *Mrs Wright* | Good mourning? Not really. I won't be happy till Harry's ashes are resting in peace. Have you done it? I hope I can rely on 'Ashes R Us'. |
| *Dribs* | Er . . . well . . . |
| *Drabs* | 'We spread your loved-one's ashes<br>Like butter on a crumpet.<br>Land or sea or air,<br>Let **Ashes R Us** dump it.' |

| | |
|---|---|
| *Dribs* | [*Glaring at Dribs*] Zip the lip. |
| *Mrs Wright* | I hope you carried out Harry's last wishes. |
| *Dribs* | Er . . . in a way. Sort of. Up to a point. You'd better sit down. [*Drabs sits down*] Not you, you idiot – Mrs Wright. |

[*Mrs Wright sits down*]

| | |
|---|---|
| *Mrs Wright* | Harry wanted his ashes looked after well. |
| *Dribs* | Did your husband write it in his will, Mrs Wright? |
| *Mrs Wright* | He only wrote a short will. 'Being of sound mind, I've spent all my money.' His mind was going. |
| *Dribs* | He was a good age. |
| *Drabs* | True. His ashes looked very wrinkled. |
| *Mrs Wright* | He was a war baby, you know. His parents took one look at him and started fighting. |
| *Dribs* | Just get the empty urn for Mrs Wright. I'm sure you'd like it back. |
| *Drabs* | Of course. Just remind me. What was it like? |
| *Mrs Wright* | It was in the shape of a car. Dear Harry loved cars. He used to change the oil every day and his shirt every 10,000 miles. |

| | |
|---|---|
| *Drabs* | Was he a good driver? |
| *Mrs Wright* | Not really. I came home one day and found the car in the lounge. When I asked him how he got it there he said: 'Easy. I just turned left at the kitchen.' |
| *Dribs* | I expect you've got lots of fond memories. |
| *Mrs Wright* | Not really. Harry wasn't easy to live with. |
| *Drabs* | Is that why he stabbed himself a hundred times? |
| *Mrs Wright* | No. He didn't know how to switch off the electric carving knife. |
| *Dribs* | I'm so sorry. |
| *Mrs Wright* | Not as sorry as I was. I was looking forward to that leg of lamb. |
| *Drabs* | You must have been so upset. |
| *Mrs Wright* | I was. In the end I had to open a tin of beans. |
| *Dribs* | At least your husband is now at peace. |
| *Mrs Wright* | So am I. He never stopped moaning. |
| *Drabs* | What about? |
| *Mrs Wright* | My rock cakes. |
| *Dribs* | I'm sure they're very nice. Didn't he like them? |

| | |
|---|---|
| *Mrs Wright* | That was the trouble. I couldn't get him to eat them. Harry was my sixth husband. The first five died after eating my rock cakes |
| *Dribs* | What a tragic story, Mrs Wright. |
| *Drabs* | It brings a lump to my throat. |
| Mr Wright | That's what they all said just before they died. |
| *Dribs* | And we were happy to do their ashes for you. |
| *Mrs Wright* | You got it all wrong before. I told you on the phone I wanted their ashes put down to rest. Not put down a vest. |
| *Drabs* | It was a crackly line. |
| *Dribs* | Get Mrs Wright a nice cup of tea. Then we can settle the bill. |
| *Drabs* | How much are we going to pay her? |
| *Dribs* | Shut up and get the tea. [*Drabs exits*] |
| *Mrs Wright* | I miss Harry. I've got a photo here. Bless him. There he is in the desert. He's sitting on a camel. |
| *Drabs* | [*Putting his head round the door*] One lump or two? |
| *Mrs Wright* | Twenty. Two on the camel and the rest on his behind. |

27

| | |
|---|---|
| *Dribs* | I'm sure your husband was a good man, Mrs Wright. |
| *Mrs Wright* | Not really. Harry spent more time in the pub than at home. That's why I asked you to scatter his ashes in the garden of the Dog and Gun. |
| *Drabs* | [*Putting his head round the door*] A very nice pub. |
| *Mrs Wright* | So did you do it? |
| *Dribs* | Er . . . Not quite, Mrs Wright. |
| *Mrs Wright* | 'No quite' – what do you mean – 'Not quite?' |
| *Drabs* | [*Putting his head round the door*] There was a mix up. |
| *Dribs* | Only a little problem. |
| *Mrs Wright* | I hope you've done as I told you. If not, he'll come back and haunt this place. |
| *Dribs* | Oh dear. |
| *Drabs* | [*Enters with tray*] I don't like to say anything but the cake just flew through the air and fell on the floor. |
| *Dribs* | It must be a poltergeist. |
| *Drabs* | No. It's a lemon sponge. I've picked it all up and brushed off most of the bits. |
| *Mrs Wright* | What bits? |

| | |
|---|---|
| Drab | Ash. Old Mr Kipling's ashes are on the kitchen floor. |
| *Mrs Wright* | I'm not eating cake covered in Mr Kipling's ashes! |
| *Drabs* | I don't see why not. They say Mr Kipling makes very good cakes. |
| *Dribs* | I think we'll just have the tea. Here's your cup, Mrs Wright. Help yourself to sugar. |
| *Mrs Wright* | [*Stirring spoonfuls into her cup*] This place is a shambles. I should have gone to 'Ash and Carry'. They never make blunders there. |
| *Dribs* | I'm sure we can put things right, Mrs Wright. |
| *Drabs* | The customer is never wrong, Mrs Wright. |
| *Mrs Wright* | [*Sipping tea and pulling a face*] Agh! What a nasty cup of tea. It tastes like soot. |
| *Drabs* | That will be the sugar. |
| *Mrs Wright* | It doesn't taste like sugar. |
| *Drabs* | That's because it's not the sugar bowl. You've just stirred two heaped spoonfuls of the old mayor into your tea. |
| *Dribs* | We'll just put his urn out of the way. And here's your empty urn back, Mrs Wright. |

| | |
|---|---|
| *Mrs Wright* | This isn't Harry's urn. This one's shaped like a star. Harry's was shaped like a car. |
| *Drabs* | I can explain. |
| *Dribs* | No! You've done enough damage. |
| *Drabs* | You see, the thing was, Mrs Wright . . . |
| *Dribs* | There were two. |
| *Mrs Wright* | Two? Two what? |
| *Dribs* | Two Mr Wrights. |
| *Drabs* | We had two urns. One was Harry Wright. The other was Larry Wright. And Larry and Harry got . . . er . . . |
| *Mrs Wright* | Mixed up? So where's my Harry? |
| *Dribs* | The beer garden at The Baker and Bun. |
| *Mrs Wright* | Not the Dog and Gun? |
| *Dribs* | No. The wrong Wright's at the Dog and Gun. Larry. |
| *Drabs* | Not your Harry. |
| *Mrs Wright* | Oh no. [*She takes out a hankie*] Harry hated the Baker and Bun. He was thrown out of there six times. Can't you get him back? |
| *Drabs* | He's . . . spread out . . . all over the beer garden. |
| *Mrs Wright* | Well get down there and sweep him up! |

| | |
|---|---|
| *Dribs* | It's not that simple. |
| *Mrs Wright* | All I want is the right Mr Wright, my Harry. Not the wrong Mr Wright – Larry. |
| *Drabs* | Yes, but . . . |
| *Mrs Wright* | No buts! Sweep him up and take him to the Dog and Gun. That will put everything right. Right? |
| *Dribs* | No quite. |
| *Mrs Wright* | What's the problem? |
| *Drabs* | It's the Wongs. |
| *Mrs Wright* | What Wongs? |
| *Dribs* | Harry and Larry Wong. They had the take-away next to the Dog and Bun. |
| *Mrs Wright* | Stop! What **are** you talking about? |
| *Drabs* | I'll explain. |
| *Dribs* | No way. I'll explain. The Wongs were twins, Mrs Wright. They both died, last week – aged 103. They wanted their ashes scattered in the beer garden of the Dog and Bun. |
| *Drabs* | But I made a mistake. |
| *Mrs Wright* | Wait a minute. You said you mixed up two Wrights. Where are the Wongs? |
| *Drabs* | I scattered them at the **Baker** and Bun, by mistake. |

| | |
|---|---|
| *Drabs* | So you can see our problem. It's very windy today. |
| Mr Wright | What's the wind got to do with it? |
| *Dribs* | It means we've got the right Wright at the Baker and Bun, all mixed up with two Wongs. |
| Mrs Wright | And where's the wrong Wright? |
| *Drabs* | Larry Wright's where Harry Wright **should** be. |
| *Dribs* | The Gun and Baker. |
| Mrs Wright | Don't you mean the Bun and Dog? |
| *Dribs* | Do I? |
| Mrs Wright | [*Dabbing her eyes with her hankie*] Poor Larry. |
| *Dribs* | [*Gently*] Don't you mean 'Poor Harry'? |
| Mrs Wright | Do I? I don't know what I mean. [*Getting up to leave*] It was a big mistake coming here. |
| *Drabs* | I'm sure we can put things right, Mrs Wong. |
| *Dribs* | [*Whispers*] Wright, not Wong. |
| Mrs Wright | No. You're wrong. You can't put it right now. After all, in your case two Wongs will never make a Wright! |